SECRETS OF THE RAINFOREST

PLANTS AND PLANTEATERS

BY MICHAEL CHINERY

CHERRYTREE BOOKS

A Cherrytree Book

Designed and produced by
A S Publishing

First published 2000
by Cherrytree Press
327 High Street
Slough
Berkshire
SL1 1TX

British Library Cataloguing in Publication Data

Chinery, Michael
Plants and planteaters. — (Secrets of the rainforest)
1.Rain forest plants — Juvenile literature
2.Herbivores — Juvenile literature
3.Rain forest animals — Juvenile literature
I.Title
591.7'34

ISBN 1 842 34001 8

Design: Richard Rowan
Artwork: Malcolm Porter
Consultant: Sue Fogden

Printed in Hong Kong by Wing King
Tong Co. Ltd

Acknowledgements
Photographs: *All by courtesy of Michael & Patricia*
Fogden with the following exceptions:
BBC Natural History Unit 9 top, 22, 22/23 top, 24, 25,
26/27 bottom, 28, 29

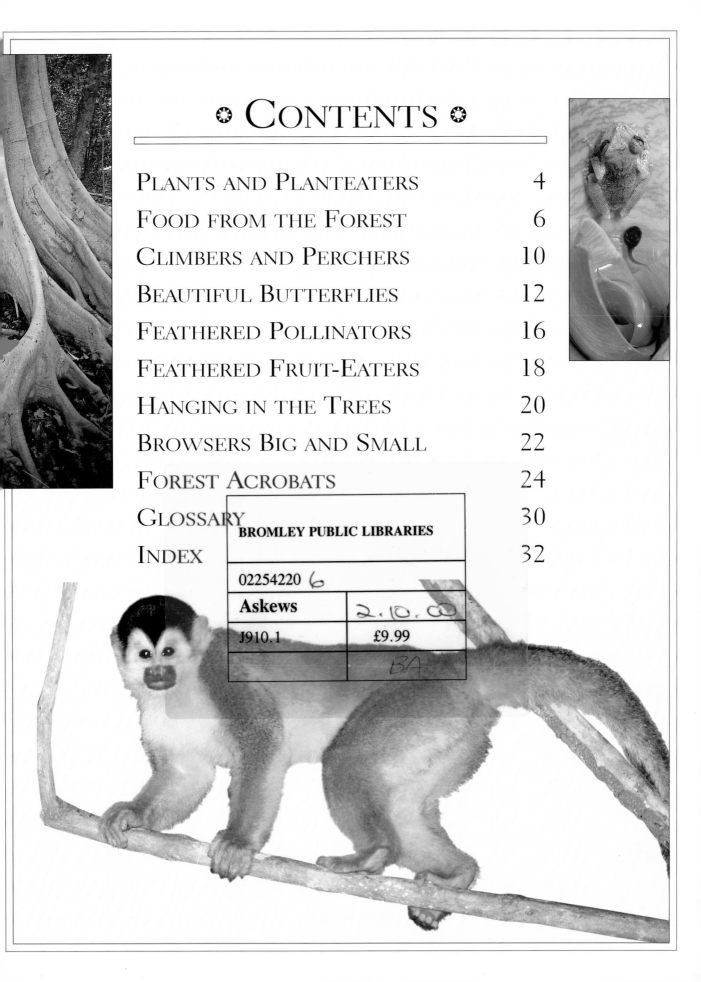

❂ CONTENTS ❂

❖ PLANTS AND PLANTEATERS ❖

TROPICAL RAINFORESTS grow in parts of the world where it is very hot as well as very wet (see map page 31). They need average temperatures above 25°C every month, and they need at least 200 cm of rain every year. These conditions occur only near to the equator – in the region that we call the tropics.

The wettest tropical rainforests get heavy rain almost every day, some drenched with over 600 cm in a year. The trees growing in them stay green all through the year. Forests growing further from the equator generally get less rain, and for a few weeks they may not get more than an occasional shower. Some of the trees growing in them are deciduous; they drop their leaves in the drier season.

CARPETS OF TREES

The trees in a tropical rainforest grow so close together that from the air the forest looks like a green carpet. But this carpet is about 30 metres above the ground. Some trees are even taller and stand above the others like giant umbrellas.

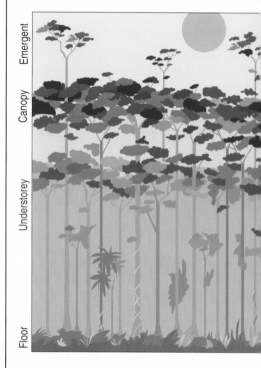

▲ The layers of a rainforest.

▼ This rainforest in Central America is shrouded with mist for much of the time. It is called a cloud forest. Everything is dripping wet, but these conditions are ideal for plant growth.

▶ Many different kinds of hummingbirds feed at flowers in the American rainforests.

Forest Layers

THE MOST important layer in the rainforest is the canopy. This is a dense layer of spreading leaves and branches, forming the roof of the forest between 25 and 35 metres above the ground. It is the factory or powerhouse of the forest, where almost all of its food and energy is produced. Most of the forest's flowers and fruits grow here, and most of the animals live here as well. Here and there, a few trees grow way above the canopy, like towers sticking up from the roof. They are called emergents and in the Asian forests some of them reach heights of about 70 metres. Below the canopy there is usually an understorey of smaller trees with narrow crowns. Many of these are young trees trying to reach the canopy. Nearer to the ground there are ferns and small flowering plants and perhaps a few scattered bushes.

It is quite dark inside the rainforest because the canopy of overhead branches shuts out most of the light. It is also very quiet and still, because not much wind penetrates the canopy. Not many plants can grow on the gloomy forest floor, so it is usually quite easy to walk through the rainforest. Dense 'jungle' develops only along the river banks and where big trees have fallen and allowed light to reach the ground.

Amazing Variety

Tropical rainforests are the richest places on earth for plant and animal life. Biologists believe that more than half of the world's plant and animal species live in these forests. The American rainforest is particularly rich in biodiversity. Over one third of the world's bird species live there. A hectare of South American rainforest may contain over a hundred different kinds of trees. You would be lucky to find five different kinds of trees in a hectare of European woodland. One reason for the richness of the forests is the fact that they are very old. They have existed for millions of years, unaffected by the ice ages and other climatic changes that have periodically destroyed forests in other parts of the world.

◀ Not all rainforests grow in hot, tropical areas. As long as there is enough rain, they can grow in cooler places. This rainforest, with lots of tree ferns, is in southeastern Australia, well outside the tropics.

☀ FOOD FROM THE FOREST ☀

TREES AND OTHER green plants all make food by a wonderful process called photosynthesis. The word means 'making by light', and the process takes place only in sunlight. In the rainforest, it nearly all takes place in the sunlit canopy. The green colouring matter in the leaves soaks up the sun's energy and uses it to combine water – from all the rain – with a gas called carbon dioxide taken from the air. The process produces sugar, which the trees then mix with minerals from

▼ This fallen tree shows what shallow roots the rainforest trees have, and also how far they spread from the base of the trunk.

FIRM ANCHORS

. . . .

RAINFOREST soils are usually rather shallow and the trees need to spread their roots over a wide area to get a good grip. Many of the larger rainforest trees have massive roots called buttress roots. These look like walls growing out from the bases of the trunks (left). They are particularly common on the biggest trees that grow above the canopy and get buffeted by the wind. The buttresses stop them from being blown over.

Stilt roots sprout from near the bases of some tree trunks and grow down into the soil. They act like sturdy guy ropes to hold the trees firmly in the ground. The original base of the tree may rot away, but the upper part lives on, supported entirely by its stilt roots. Stilt roots occur mainly on the smaller trees and especially on those growing in waterlogged soils.

the soil to make all the things they need for their growth. If there were not so much rain, the rainforest trees would not be able to grow so fast and so tall.

▲ Caterpillars like this monarch butterfly larva are eating machines, devouring twice their weight every day.

The food that the trees make provides food for the forest animals. Some eat the leaves, some the nectar from the flowers, some the fruit, some the seeds. Because it is warm all year, rather than in a single season, there is a continuous supply of flowers, fruits and seeds.

Some insects and birds have special adaptations that allow them to feed from just one particular kind of flower. In return the animals carry pollen from flower to flower and help them produce seeds. In some cases the relationship between plant and animal is so close that neither could survive without the other.

FOOD CHAINS

The forest plants provide food for the planteating animals, and the planteating animals in turn become food for the meateating animals that prey on them. An ant may eat a plant's seeds and be eaten by a bird which is eaten by a cat. This is an example of a simple food chain. There are many complicated food chains in a rainforest but they all depend on plants. When an animal dies, its body decays and returns to the soil. The goodness in it is used by the plants, and so the cycle continues.

THE FOREST FLOOR

The floor of the rainforest is dark, damp and very warm, although not as hot as neighbouring areas outside the forest. Decay is rapid under these conditions and dead leaves rarely accumulate on the ground as they do in the temperate woodlands of Europe and North America. Rainforest soils are therefore rather thin. Fungi and microscopic bacteria quickly rot the fallen leaves. Giant snails and pencil-sized millipedes with hundreds of legs also munch their way through the dead leaves and fallen fruit. Termites and beetles make short work of fallen twigs and other timber. The plant-eating animals of the forest floor provide lots of food for predatory creatures, such as scorpions and centipedes. Many birds also feed on the forest floor. Some eat only fallen fruits and seeds, but most of them eat insects and other small animals as well.

WATERY FORESTS

Where rainforests sweep down to the sea or to river mouths, big trees give way to shorter ones called mangroves that grow in the mud between high and low tide levels. These

HOUSE PLANTS

NOT many plants can grow on the forest floor because the canopy cuts out most of the light that they need to make their food. The plants that do grow there commonly have dark leaves, often tinged with red or purple. These darker colours help the leaves to absorb the light more efficiently. Several of the plants adapted for life on the forest floor make good house plants because they can cope with low light levels indoors. The African violet (above) is a good example.

GIANT FLOWER

THE world's biggest flower is called rafflesia. It may be as much as a metre across and weigh up to 7 kg. The plant is a parasite that steals all its food from a liana (see page 10). Hair-like threads growing inside the roots and stems of the liana soak up food and then form a flower bud. The bud bursts through the stem of the liana at ground level and opens after several weeks. The flower (left) smells of rotting flesh and this attracts small flies that do the work of pollination. Rafflesia is an endangered species, growing only on the islands of Borneo and Sumatra in Southeast Asia.

▼ Curassows live in the forests of tropical America. They feed mainly on fruit and insects. Smaller species feed in the trees but larger ones, including this Salvin's curassow, feed mainly on the ground.

FISHES IN THE FOREST

Parts of the Amazon rainforest are flooded for about six months of the year. The rivers carry so much water at this time that they burst their banks. Water up to 10 metres deep floods into the forest and takes the river life with it. The fig tree (left) is growing in one of these flooded areas. Fishes take the place of birds, exploring the tree trunks and submerged plants, and feeding on falling fruits and seeds. Insects and spiders have to climb up into the canopy, but many of them fall and these are also eaten by the fishes.

areas are called mangrove swamps. Tangled roots like upturned baskets anchor the trees firmly in the mud and prevent the tides from sweeping them away. Oxygen is in short supply in the waterlogged mud, so many mangroves have special breathing roots that stick up from the mud. When the tide is out they look like forests of pencils.

Mangrove swamps are full of animals. Many small creatures feed on the leaves or on the debris trapped around the tree roots. Bigger animals, including snakes and crocodiles, feed on the small ones.

The seeds of some mangrove trees germinate before they fall from the branches. A tough, pointed root grows down from the seed and the whole thing looks like a thick dart, up to 50 cm long. When the seed eventually falls, the root is driven far into the mud. Firmly anchored in this way, the seedling starts to grow immediately, with no risk of being washed away by the tide.

❀ CLIMBERS AND PERCHERS ❀

RAINFORESTS ARE full of climbing plants called lianas. Almost every tree has at least one liana wrapped around it. A liana begins life as a seed sprouting on the forest floor. Its slender, snake-like stem sprawls over the ground until it finds a tree or a bush that it can climb. Twining around the trunk or sprawling over the branches, the liana grows rapidly upwards towards the canopy. Once it reaches the sunlight, it produces flowers and fruits just like the surrounding trees. Lianas also send out lots of wiry branches that snake from tree to tree and bind them all together in a dense network. Many of these branches drop down to the ground before finding another tree to climb. Apes and monkeys find these 'bush-ropes' convenient for swinging through the forest.

AIR PLANTS

Not all rainforest plants grow in the soil. Many of them grow on the trunks and branches of the trees. These perching plants are called epiphytes. They include many beautiful orchids as well as ferns and plants called bromeliads, which are relatives of the pineapple. The tiny seeds of orchids and the spores of ferns are

◀ Lianas hang down from the forest canopy and twine around the tree trunks like thick ropes.

TREE-TOP SWAMPS

THE canopy of a rainforest with lots of bromeliads and stag's-horn ferns is in some ways like a swamp because the plants hold so much water in their crowns of leaves. Hundreds of different kinds of tree frogs (right) breed in these tree-top pools. Most of them spend all their lives in the trees and never come down to the ground. Suction pads on their toes help them cling to the shiny leaves. Many mosquitoes also breed in the tree-top pools and their wriggly larvae provide food for the frogs' tadpoles. Colourful worms called flatworms also live in the tree-top swamps and glide over the wet leaves and branches in search of food.

▼ Clinging tightly to a tree trunk, these clusters of epiphytic ferns hold stores of water at the bases of their leaves.

▼ Small epiphytic palms almost completely conceal the tree trunk on which they are growing.

▶ Perching in the canopy, this is one of thousands of epiphytic orchids growing in the world's rainforests.

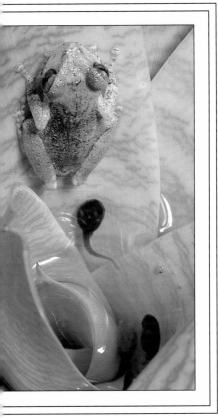

blown into bark crevices by the wind. Larger seeds may be dropped by animals and they take root in the dead leaves and other debris trapped on the branches.

Epiphytes are sometimes called air plants because they seem to exist only on the air, but they actually grow just like other plants. Getting water is no problem because it is all around the plants. Many orchids have spongy roots that hang freely in the air and soak up the rain that falls on them. Bromeliads and many ferns have cup-like leaf bases that catch the rain. Minerals come from the dead leaves and animal droppings trapped around the bases of the plants. Epiphytes do not take food from the trees and normally do them no harm, although if there are too many epiphytes their weight may bring the branches crashing down.

STRANGLER FIGS

STRANGLING figs of one kind or another grow in all the rainforests. A strangler starts life as an epiphyte. Its seed germinates on the branch of a rainforest tree, but it soon sends long roots snaking down the trunk and into the ground. These take water and minerals from the soil like those of any other tree. They branch and thicken, and eventually surround the trunk of the supporting tree like a cage (left). At the same time, the foliage of the fig grows thick and strong and smothers the leaves of the supporting tree. The tree gradually dies and rots away, leaving the strangler growing in its place.

PLANTS THAT EAT INSECTS

PITCHER plants have leaves designed to trap insects. The leaf is like a jug or pitcher with a lid at the end. With the lid open the trap is set. Sugary nectar around the pitcher rim attracts flies and other insects. Once they set foot on the inside of the pitcher they are doomed. Unable to get a grip on the waxy surface, they slide down into the pool of digestive juices inside the pitcher. These juices are produced by the walls of the pitcher and they quickly reduce the insects to empty shells. The digested flesh of the insects is soaked up by the walls of the pitcher and used to feed the whole plant.

☸ BEAUTIFUL BUTTERFLIES ☸

THOUSANDS OF different trees and other plants grow in the rainforest and their flowers provide nectar for thousands of different kinds of butterflies. Whatever the time of year, there are always some plants in flower. Most of the flowers are high up in the canopy and most of the butterflies live there as well. They include the world's biggest and most colourful butterflies, some of which glide over the canopy on wings up to 28 cm across.

QUICK CHANGES

The year-round warmth enables the rainforest butterflies to produce several generations, or broods, every year. Some species can grow from egg to adult in just three

▼ The common birdwing, widely distributed in southern Asia, has a wingspan of over 15 cm, but some of its relatives are nearly twice as big.

▶ Caterpillars eat tonnes of leaves in the rainforest but are themselves eaten in their hundreds of thousands.

weeks, whereas insects living in the cooler parts of the world generally need a whole year to complete their life cycles. Evolution, which is the process by which plants and animals gradually change from one generation to another, can therefore take place much more quickly among the tropical insects than among those living in cooler areas. This is probably why there are so many more insect species in the tropical forests than in the cooler parts of the world.

► Owl butterflies get their name from the large eye-like markings on their wings. Up to 20 cm across their outstretched wings, these butterflies fly mainly at dusk and are often mistaken for moths.

FUSSY EATERS

When a butterfly lays her eggs, she is very particular where she lays them. Only one type of plant will do for each type of butterfly. The tiny eggs grow into larvae called caterpillars. The caterpillars feed on the plants they are born on and will eat no others. The leaf-munching caterpillars are often so numerous that their droppings fall like rain. Some droppings reach the forest floor, but many are caught up in the branches and they help to nourish the perching plants, or epiphytes, growing there.

NECTAR DRINKERS

Butterflies feed mainly on nectar and other sweet liquids, including the juices of over-ripe fruits. Some butterflies also like to drink sap oozing from tree trunks. They suck the liquids through a tongue called a proboscis, which is just like a very thin drinking straw. When the tongue is not in use it is rolled up underneath the head.

BUTTERFLY JEWELS

SOUTH America's morpho butterflies are famous for their dazzling blue wings. Up to 20 cm across, they include some of the most brilliant of the rainforest butterflies. It is usually just the males that have these brilliant colours. Most of the females are brown. Morphos feed mainly on over-ripe or rotting fruit rather than on nectar.

GLASSWING BUTTERFLIES

A BUTTERFLY'S wings are normally covered with tiny, overlapping scales, rather like the tiles on a roof. The scales give the butterfly its beautiful colours. The wings of some South American butterflies have so few scales that you can see right through them. In the forest it is not easy for birds and other enemies to see these glasswing butterflies at all.

▶ Swallowtail butterflies get their name from the little tails at the rear of their hindwings. Dozens of species live in the rainforests though many have become rare because their forest homes have been destroyed. This green-spotted swallowtail comes from Southeast Asia and tropical parts of Australia.

MUDDY FEASTS

● ● ● ● ● ● ● ● ● ● ● ● ● ● ● ● ● ●

MUDDY patches on river banks or in other more open parts of the rainforest often attract huge numbers of butterflies, belonging to many different species. Hundreds or even thousands of butterflies crowd together as they try to push their tongues into the mud. This behaviour is called mud-puddling, but the butterflies are not looking for water – there is plenty of that in the rainforest. They are eager to find mineral salts, which they need for the proper working of their reproductive systems. It is sometimes possible to get quite close to the mud-puddling butterflies, but if one insect is alarmed and flies up the others usually follow in a dazzling, multicoloured cloud.

Nearly all the mud-puddlers are male butterflies, and because of this it was once thought that the females of many rainforest butterflies were very rare. In fact, males and females are equally common, but the females usually stay out of sight in the canopy. Unlike the males, they do not need to gather mineral salts.

☸ FEATHERED POLLINATORS ☸

FLOWERS MUST be pollinated before they can form seeds. Pollen has to be transferred from one flower to another of the same kind. Birds, bats and insects all help to pollinate rainforest flowers. Birds are attracted by the bright colours of the flowers and they drink their sugary nectar. While drinking they get dusted with pollen, some of which they carry to the next flower. In the tropics birds can find flowers at all times of the year, and many of them have become specialist nectar-feeders. They usually have long slender beaks for reaching the nectar deep inside the flowers. Nectar-feeding birds cannot live in the cooler parts of the world because there are not many flowers in the winter.

COLOURFUL HUMMINGBIRDS

Hummingbirds have beautiful, shiny feathers and they look like jewels as they dart from flower to flower. Many different kinds live in the American rainforests. Their slender beaks are sometimes longer than the rest of the body, and their tongues are even longer. The tongue is curled from side to side to form a tube for gathering the nectar. The birds can

HONEY-EATERS, LORIES AND LORIKEETS

HONEY-EATERS live in the forests of New Guinea and surrounding areas. They do not all have long beaks, but they do

have long tongues for gathering nectar. The tongue soaks up nectar with its brush-like tip and the nectar runs into a deep groove. When the tongue is pulled back into the beak, the nectar is squeezed out and swallowed. Some honey-eaters can poke their tongues out more than 15 times in a second to soak up the nectar.

Lories and lorikeets are small parrots. They have much shorter tongues than other nectar-feeding birds and visit flowers with shorter petal-tubes. A tuft of hair at the tip of the tongue mops up the nectar and pollen. The birds sometimes eat whole flowers and small fruits. Several different kinds of lories and lorikeets live in the rainforests of New Guinea and neighbouring areas. This one is a rainbow lorikeet.

hover in front of the flowers while sucking out the nectar, and they can also fly backwards. Flexible shoulder joints allow their wings to whirr round like tiny propellers at up to 100 times a second, giving out the humming sound for which the birds are named.

Hummingbirds drink up to nine times their own weight of nectar each day, and to get this they have to visit about 2000 flowers. Most of them are attracted to red flowers.

▲ The white-tipped sicklebill (top right) is a very specialised hummingbird. Its beak is perfectly adapted to sip nectar from the curved heliconia flowers, but it cannot get nectar from other flowers.

◀ Hovering on tiny wings, this coppery-headed emerald hummingbird dips its beak into a flower with perfect aim.

▶ Wings whirring like propellers keep this green violetear hummingbird in position under the flowers.

✻ FEATHERED FRUIT-EATERS ✻

MANY RAINFOREST birds specialise in eating fruit and rarely eat anything else. This is possible in a rainforest because there are so many different kinds of trees, and fruit is available all through the year. Birds living in cooler parts of the world can eat fruit only in summer and autumn, and have to find other foods in winter and spring. The beaks or bills of the rainforest birds are wonderfully adapted for picking and opening the many different kinds of fruits.

TOP-HEAVY TOUCANS

Toucans look top-heavy because their colourful beaks are so big – sometimes as long as the rest of the body. But their beaks are actually very light because they are hollow. The large beaks enable the birds to reach fruits hanging from the tips of slender branches. When it has picked a fruit, a toucan throws its head back and the fruit rolls down into its throat.

▼ Toucans wave their beaks about like flags to signal to each other. This is a keel-billed toucan from Costa Rica.

▼ The Australian king parrot (below centre) uses its strong beak to crush seeds. It also crushes flowers to drink their nectar.

The Dazzling Quetzal

THE quetzal lives in the forests of Central America. The long, shiny feathers streaming from its wings and tail are up to a metre long. The male has a bright red belly, but the rest of its feathers are green and the bird is not easy to see in the forest canopy. Its favourite fruit is the avocado, whose oil-rich flesh provides it with plenty of energy. Although wild avocados are not as big as the ones that we eat, a single fruit still makes quite a mouthful for the pigeon-sized quetzal. The bird flies straight at the avocado with its beak open and relies on its speed and weight to break the fruit from its stalk. The fruit is swallowed whole and the bird spits out the hard woody stone later.

Living Nutcrackers

Parrots live in many parts of the world and in many habitats. Macaws are noisy parrots living in the forests of South America. Their powerful, hooked beaks can easily open the thick, woody shells of Brazil nuts. The birds also use their beaks like extra feet to cling to the branches while they are climbing.

▲ Macaws often eat poisonous seeds, but come to no harm because they also eat clay from river banks. The clay soaks up the poisons in the birds' stomachs.

◄ The green honeycreeper lives in Central America and feeds on flowers and fruits. It helps the plants by scattering their seeds while feeding.

✸ HANGING IN THE TREES ✸

MANY TREE-TOP mammals move about by hanging or swinging from the branches instead of walking along them. Some of them can wrap their tails around the branches and use them as extra legs. Most of these tree-dwellers feed on fruits and seeds, but sloths and a few others specialise in eating leaves.

LIFE UPSIDE DOWN

The slowest of all mammals, sloths rarely move. Mostly they simply hang upside down in the sunshine, holding on to a branch with their big, curved claws. They sleep for up to 20 hours a day and use up so little energy that they can manage on a diet of leaves, which they digest very slowly. Sloths do everything slowly and may take a month to digest a large meal. Their long fur usually looks green because tiny plants called algae grow on the hairs. The plants help to camouflage the sloths in the canopy and hide them from harpy eagles and other predators.

TREE-TOP GLIDERS

Some pouched mammals can glide from one tree to another: a fold of skin opens out to form a wing on each side of the body when the animals stretch their legs. The Australian sugar glider can glide for up to 50 metres, with its bushy tail

▼ Sloths make no homes. The mother sloth has one baby at a time and carries it around on her belly for up to nine months.

KANGAROOS IN THE TREES
. . . .
THERE are no native monkeys or squirrels in New Guinea or Australia. Their role as tree-top feeders is filled by tree kangaroos and various other pouched mammals. Tree kangaroos feed on leaves in the rainforests of New Guinea. They

look more like monkeys or squirrels than kangaroos because they do not have such big back legs as other kangaroos. But their back legs are still very strong and the animals can make enormous leaps from one tree to another. Like the tree kangaroos, the dwarf cuscus (above) is a marsupial. It carries its babies in a pouch at first. Living mainly in the understorey of the Indonesian rainforest, it feeds largely on fruit although it also eats plenty of insects.

SWEET-TOOTHED KINKAJOUS

KINKAJOUS look like monkeys as they swing through the canopy and hang from the branches by their long tails. But they are more closely related to bears and racoons. Although they climb well, they do not leap from branch to branch like monkeys. They do not let go of one branch until they have a firm grip on another. Kinkajous live in tropical America. Most of their relatives are flesh-eaters, but kinkajous prefer fruit. Kinkajous also like honey and get it by poking their long tongues into the nests of wild bees. The kinkajou's tongue is about 15 cm long – about one third as long as its body. Big eyes help the animal to see well at night.

THE PECULIAR HOATZIN

THE hoatzin of South America is a peculiar bird. It cannot fly well and usually just glides from tree to tree. Baby hoatzins leave their nests at a very early stage and clamber about in the canopy with the aid of two hooked claws on each wing. Hoatzins feed mainly on leaves, especially those of the epiphytic plants growing in the canopy.

acting as a rudder. It gets its name from its habit of biting into bark and lapping up the sugary sap that flows from the wounds.

FRUIT-EATING BATS

Fruit bats are also called flying foxes because many of them have fox-like faces and all of them can fly. Their wings stretch from their shoulders to the tips of their long fingers and back to the tail. They are up to two metres across. The bats sleep upside down in the trees by day, with their wings wrapped tightly around their bodies, and wake up to feed at dusk. They feed mainly on ripe fruit, but some of the smaller kinds drink nectar. Fruit bats live in many of the warmer parts of the world, but not in America. Many thousands of them may gather to sleep in one small area.

✦ Browsers Big and Small ✦

NOT MANY large planteating mammals live on the rainforest floor because there are not a lot of plants for them to eat. The browsing mammals that do live there usually live alone or in small family groups and they are generally very shy and secretive. They are most likely to be found in the dense vegetation that grows along the river banks and in the forest clearings. They find plenty of tender leaves near the ground in these areas. Although they feed mainly on leaves, browsing mammals often add fallen fruit to their diet.

Size Matters

Most of the forest browsers are either deer or antelopes, or pigs. These forest dwellers are generally much smaller than their grassland cousins. Large size can be an advantage in open country, but it is a disadvantage in dense vegetation. The Javan and Sumatran rhinos of Southeast Asia, for example, are much smaller than other rhinos. The pygmy hippopotamus is so much smaller than the true hippo that it is easily mistaken for a baby hippo.

Antelopes and Deer

THE African bongo (left) is the largest rainforest antelope. It is not much more than a metre high, but it weighs up to 400 kg and, with its horns laid back over its shoulders, it can easily crash through dense vegetation. The royal antelope of the West African rainforests is the smallest of all antelopes. It is only 30 cm high and weighs only 2.5 kg. The northern pudu is the smallest of the world's deer. It lives in the dense rainforests on the slopes of the Andes Mountains in the northern part of South America. It is no more than 40 cm high and has tiny spikes for antlers. Deer antlers and antelope horns are usually quite small in forest-living species, so they do not get tangled up in the vegetation.

▼ The okapi's stripes help to camouflage the animal by breaking up its outline.

STURDY TAPIRS AND AGOUTIS

TAPIRS (above) are related to both horses and rhinos. Their sturdy bodies, weighing up to 300 kg, are perfectly built for forcing their way through the dense vegetation of river banks and forest clearings. The animals feed mainly on leaves and twigs, which they pull down with their short trunks. They also eat grass and waterplants.

Agoutis are sturdy South American rodents, not unlike long-legged guinea pigs. They eat some leaves, but feed mainly on fallen fruit. They listen for the thud of fruits falling to the ground and then rush out to find them. People often hunt the animals by throwing stones, which the agoutis think are falling fruits. Their teeth are strong enough and sharp enough to gnaw through the woody shells of Brazil nuts.

The Indian, or Asiatic, elephant is the largest of all rainforest animals. It grows to a height of about 3 metres and weighs up to 5 tonnes, but it is still much smaller than the elephants living on the African savannas. Smaller still are the forest elephants living in the rainforests of western and central Africa. These are under 2.5 metres high and are darker and hairier than savanna elephants.

The okapi is one of the tallest forest browsers. It is related to the giraffe and grows to a height of nearly 2.5 metres. It lives deep in the rainforests of Central Africa and was not discovered until 1901. Even now, few people have ever seen an okapi.

SIGHT AND SOUND

Sounds and scents are more important than sight in the dim forests. It is not so easy for animals to see through the trees, so they call to each other instead. Most of the mammals have large ears and a good sense of smell. Asiatic and forest elephants are noticeably noisier than bush elephants that live in open country and can see each other coming.

◀ South America's collared peccary is related to pigs. It feeds mainly on roots.

⚜ FOREST ACROBATS ⚜

GIBBONS AND orang-utans are apes that live in Southeast Asia. Gibbons live in small family groups in the tree-tops. They are among the fastest and noisiest of the mammals in the tree-tops. When they wake up in the morning they spend an hour or so hooting loudly. The calls can be heard all over the forest and they let other gibbon families know that the area is occupied and that they should keep away.

Gibbons feed mainly on fruit, and when they find a tree with a good crop of fruit they get very excited. They start hooting again to make sure that other gibbon families stay away from the feast. Gibbons also eat small amounts of leaves and flowers, as well as occasional lizards and other small animals.

OLD MAN OF THE FOREST

The orang-utan lives only on the islands of Borneo and Sumatra. Its name means 'old man of the forest'. Adult males have wrinkled faces and greyish beards and some of them really do look like old men.

▲ A gibbon opens its mouth wide to make its early morning calls.

▼ To start with, gibbon babies are fed on milk but soon learn from their mothers how to pick fruit.

▲ A young male orang-utan. Orang-utans are seriously endangered by logging and forest fires that devastate their homes.

SWINGING THROUGH THE TREES

GIBBONS and orang-utans have arms that are longer and stronger than their legs. They move through the canopy mainly by swinging from hand to hand along the branches. This kind of movement is called brachiation and it requires very powerful shoulder muscles. Long hands and fingers give the animals a firm grip on the branches. Gibbons can move so quickly that they seem to fly through the tree-tops, sometimes covering 10 metres or more with each swing and hardly appearing to touch the branches at all. They can also walk upright along the branches, using their long arms to balance themselves.

Orang-utans (left) are bigger and heavier than gibbons and they move more slowly, but they are still wonderful acrobats. They use all four limbs to climb and swing through the branches. An orang-utan never leaps from branch to branch like a gibbon. It always hangs on with at least one hand or foot until it can get another good grip, even if this means doing the splits!

Females are smaller and less wrinkled than the males.

Orang-utans feed mainly on fruit, including hard-shelled nuts that they break open with their strong teeth. They also eat some leaves and occasionally catch small animals. Each adult wanders through a home area, or range, of several square kilometres. The ranges of neighbouring animals often overlap, but the animals rarely meet. Each one bellows loudly from time to time, especially in the mornings, and this is usually enough to keep the animals apart.

Several orang-utans may gather to feed in a particularly good tree at fruiting time, but they take little notice of each other. An orang-utan seems to know all the good trees in its area and, although it does not move very far in a day, it always manages to be in the right place when the fruit is ripe. Big males often wander over the forest floor, and make their beds there with leafy branches broken from the bushes. Other orang-utans rarely come down from the trees.

AGILE MONKEYS

Every rainforest in the world is a home for monkeys. Most of them live high in the canopy. Their feet and hands are good at gripping branches, though they tend to run and jump from branch to branch rather than swinging with their arms. Their tails help them to balance. Some South American monkeys have prehensile tails, which can be used like extra hands to grasp the branches.

Most monkeys love fruit, though they usually eat some insects and other small animals as well and they often take birds' eggs. Some monkeys, including the curious proboscis monkeys, eat only leaves. Leaves are not easy to digest and the monkeys have to eat large quantities in order to get enough food from them. They need big stomachs to hold all the leaves and they are often rather pot-bellied.

▶ Spider monkeys have long arms and legs and well deserve their name. The one on the right is drinking nectar from a flower. Notice how it has anchored itself with its long, prehensile tail.

OLD WORLD AND NEW WORLD MONKEYS

MONKEYS belong to the group of mammals called primates. This group also contains the apes and human beings, but monkeys differ from the apes in having tails. Most of them are also smaller than the apes. Monkeys living in Africa and Asia – the Old World – have narrow noses, with their nostrils close together and pointing downwards, as you can see in the crested black macaque (left). New World monkeys, from the Americas, like the silky marmoset (right), have broad noses with well-separated nostrils that face outwards.

▶ A howler monkey bellows out his warning to other howler monkeys to keep out of his clan's territory.

▼ The South American squirrel monkey has strong back legs and generally jumps from branch to branch. It feeds mainly on flowers and fruits.

MONKEYS LARGE AND SMALL

Howler monkeys eat a mixture of fruit and leaves. They are fairly slow-moving animals and spend a lot of time sitting quietly and digesting their leafy meals. Among the noisiest of animals, their howling calls can carry as much as five kilometres through the forest. A hollow bone in a big throat pouch acts like a megaphone to amplify the sound. Howlers live in groups of up to 30 animals and the howling warns other howler groups to keep away. It may also frighten ocelots and other enemies.

Howlers are the largest of the American monkeys. Fully grown animals weigh up to 10 kg. Marmosets are tiny. The pygmy marmoset, weighing under 200 g, is the smallest of all monkeys. Marmosets eat fruit and insects, especially juicy caterpillars, and sometimes catch lizards and small snakes. They also use their chisel-shaped front teeth to gouge holes in tree trunks and branches, and then they lap up the sugary sap that oozes from the holes.

The closely related tamarins have smaller front teeth and cannot chew holes in bark, but they often move in to feed when the marmosets have finished. Marmosets and tamarins have sharp claws that help them to climb smooth tree trunks. Other monkeys all have nails on their fingers and toes, just as we do.

▼ Like other monkeys, this marmoset has large forward-pointing eyes that enable it to judge distances accurately, an essential skill for animals that spend their lives leaping from branch to branch.

▶ The mandrill is a large ground-living monkey of the African rainforest. The male's colours get even brighter when it is angry.

▶ At rest on a fruit-laden branch, this white-lipped tamarin from Brazil clearly displays the claws that help it to climb.

◀ The proboscis monkey of Borneo uses its big nose to make loud hooting calls. When calling, it lifts its nose like a trumpet to increase the sound.

☀ GLOSSARY ☀

Adaptation Changes in a plant or animal that increase its ability to survive and reproduce in its particular environment.

Air plant A name sometimes given to epiphytic plants that perch on the branches of trees. They were once thought to survive purely on air. See Epiphyte.

Bacteria Microscopic single-celled organisms that exist everywhere in nature and play an important role in the break-down and recycling of dead plants and animals. Many of them, often known as germs, cause disease in living plants and animals.

Biodiversity The variety of species found in any natural region. The rainforests contain more species than any other habitat.

Birdwing One of a number of very large butterflies living in Southeast Asia.

Brachiation The name given to the movement of gibbons and some monkeys that swing through the branches with their arms.

Bromeliads A group of tropical plants, including the pineapple, with a rosette of stiff leaves. Many are epiphytes.

Buttress roots Large roots that spread from the base of a tree like low walls and help to support the trunk.

Canopy The 'roof' of the rainforest, formed by the leafy branches of the trees. It is usually about 30 metres above the ground and cuts off most of the light from the forest floor.

Carbon dioxide A gas in the air that plants use for photosynthesis.

Cloud forest Areas of forest that are so high up that they are almost permanently shrouded in mist.

Debris Fallen leaves and other matter left to decompose.

Deciduous tree Any tree that drops all of its leaves for part of the year.

Emergent Any large tree that grows above the rainforest canopy.

Endangered species Plant or animal species whose numbers have fallen so far that without protection they face extinction.

Epiphyte Any plant that grows on another, especially on the branches of a tree, but takes no food from it. Ferns, orchids and bromeliads are common epiphytes in the rainforests.

Equator The imaginary line around the centre of the earth, midway from the north and south poles.

Evergreen Any tree or shrub that remains green throughout the year.

Evolution The process by which plants and animals slowly change from generation to generation, gradually giving rise to new species that are adapted to different habitats and different ways of life.

Flying fox Any of a number of large fruit-eating bats, with faces very like those of foxes.

Fruit bat Any large bat that feeds mainly on fruit.

Fungi (singular fungus) Organisms, including mushrooms and moulds, that absorb their food from living or dead matter.

Germinate To begin to grow. A seed germinates by putting down a root and sending up a shoot.

Habitat The place where certain animals and plants normally live.

Herbivore An animal that feeds on plants.

Larva (plural larvae) A stage in the development of some animals. Caterpillars and tadpoles are larvae.

Liana A climbing plant with long, woody stems that hang from the trees like ropes. Also known as vines, lianas belong to many different plant families.

Mangrove Any of a group of small, evergreen trees with tangled, basket-like roots that grow around tropical coasts.

Minerals Chemical substances, some of which are essential for life.

Nectar The sweet, sugary juice produced by flowers and some other plant organs to attract and feed insects.

Omnivore An animal that eats both plant and animal matter.

Oxygen A gas in the air and in water that is

ENDANGERED!

R AINFORESTS are vitally important to the well-being of the world but they are in danger of destruction. Many of the animals and plants featured in this book are under threat from forest clearance. If you are interested in knowing more about rainforests and in helping to conserve them, you may find these addresses and websites useful.

Friends of the Earth, Rainforest Campaign, *26-28 Underwood Street, London N1 7JQ*

Rainforest Foundation, *A5 City Cloisters, 188-96 Old St, London EC1V 9FR*

Worldwide Fund for Nature
WWF (Australia), *Level 5, 725 George Street, Sydney, NSW 2000*
WWF (South Africa), *116 Dorp Street, Stellenbosch 7600*
WWF (UK), *Panda House, Weyside Park, Cattershall Lane, Godalming, Surrey GU17 1XR*

Worldwide Fund for Nature
http://www.wwf-uk.org

Friends of the Earth
http://www.foe.co.uk

Environmental Education Network
http://envirolink.org.enviroed/

Rainforest Foundation
http://rainforestfoundationuk.org

Rainforest Preservation Foundation
http://www.flash.net/~rpf/

Survival International
http://www.survival.org.uk

Sustainable Development
http://iisd1.iisd.ca/

Rainforest Action Network
http://www.igc.apc.org/ran/intro.html

◀ **The map shows the location of the world's main rainforest areas.**

essential to plant and animal life.

Parasite An organism that lives and feeds on another living organism, called a host.

Photosynthesis The process by which green plants make food. The plants use energy from sunlight to convert water and carbon dioxide gas into sugar.

Pitcher plant Any of several plants whose leaves form liquid-filled traps for insects.

Pollen The dust-like material formed in the stamens of flowers and carried by wind or by animals to other flowers of the same kind. This transfer is called pollination and it leads to the formation of fruits and seeds.

Pollination See Pollen.

Predator An animal that eats other live animals, its prey.

Prehensile tails Tails that can grasp, allowing their owners to hang from a branch.

Proboscis A long snout, such as an elephant's trunk or the nose of the proboscis monkey, or a butterfly's long tongue.

Savanna The vast grassy plains of Africa where there are few or no trees.

Stilt roots Slender roots growing out like guy ropes from the lower part of a tree trunk and helping to hold it up.

Territory An area inhabited and defended by an animal or group of animals against others of the same species.

Tropical Describes the tropics – the warm areas around the equator.

Trunk The main stem of a tree.

Tusk Name given to an outsized tooth in a mammal, such as an elephant or a wild pig.

Understorey The layer of vegetation growing below the canopy, consisting mainly of young trees.

☸ INDEX ☸

Page numbers in *italics* refer to illustrations.